SPEAKING TO YOU

edited by

Michael Rosen and David Jackson

MACMILLAN
EDUCATION

Selection and editorial matter © Michael Rosen and
David Jackson 1984

All rights reserved. No reproduction, copy or transmission
of this publication may be made without written permission.

No paragraph of this publication may be reproduced, copied
or transmitted save with written permission or in accordance
with the provisions of the Copyright Act 1956 (as amended),
or under the terms of any licence permitting limited copying
issued by the Copyright Licensing Agency, 33 – 4 Alfred Place,
London WC1E 7DP.

Any person who does any unauthorised act in relation to
this publication may be liable to criminal prosecution and
civil claims for damages.

First published 1984
Reprinted 1985, 1986, 1988

Published by
MACMILLAN EDUCATION LTD
Houndmills, Basingstoke, Hampshire **RG21 2XS**
and London
Companies and representatives
throughout the world

Printed in Hong Kong

British Library Cataloguing in Publication Data
Rosen, Michael
Speaking to you.
1. English poetry — 20th Century
I. Title   II. Jackson, David
821'.914'0809282   PR1225
ISBN 0-333-36360-4

Contents

To the reader
In the beginning was the word   *Tom Leonard*   8

Families
As soon as I could speak   *Debbie Carnegie*   9
Parents' sayings   *Michael Rosen*   10
I don't like my brother in the morning   *Keith Ballentine*   11
Hugger mugger   *Kit Wright*   12
Bacun rind   *Barry Heath*   14
Mum, can I go out?   *Helen Cranswick*   15
The dog lovers   *Spike Milligan*   16

School
I was walking down the stairs   *Sunny Caruana*   17
First day at school   *Roger McGough*   18
Daydream   *Deepak Kalha*   19
School   *Isaac Gordon*   20
Conversations   *Deepak Kalha*   22
The class   *Michael Rosen*   24
Napoleon   *Miroslav Holub*   26

Proving yourself
Dumb insolence   *Adrian Mitchell*   28
When I realised I wasn't so brave after all   *Alex Chaplin*   29
Wall walk   *Robert Froman*   30
Delinquent   *Langston Hughes*   31
Golden Harvest   *Liz Lochhead*   32
False friends-like   *William Barnes*   33
When I was 15   *Michael Rosen*   34
Domino   *Rose Porter*   36
Nooligan   *Roger McGough*   37

Letting your hair down
Reckless   *Pete Brown*   38
Sittn guzzlin   *Tom Leonard*   39
Fingerlicking   *Judith Ellis*   40
Accidentally   *Ishikawa Takuboku*   40
Ee shynta ducked!   *Barry Heath*   41
No swimming in the town   *Ian Serraillier*   42
Fishermen   *Anon*   43
End of a holiday   *Ian Hamilton Finlay*   44

A good time
A rock concert in Belfast *Patrick Gibson* 46
Two Rastaman *Michael Payne* 47
Dub rock *Hugh Boatswain* 48
Blues for Stevie Wonder *Sam Greenlee* 49

Race
Questionnaired *Tessa Stiven* 51
Immigrants *Sam Greenlee* 52
Ballad of the landlord *Langston Hughes* 54
Harassment *Frederick Williams* 56
The 100 Centre Street, boy, you better dress up neat blues
  Anon 58

He and she
First kiss *Adam Pritchard* 59
Would you believe it *Mick Gowar* 60
When we met I said *Michael Rosen* 61
He and she *R.D. Laing* 62

The role of women
Advert *Anon* 63
Poem for my sister *Liz Lochhead* 64
Let us now praise fearful men *Michelene Wandor* 65
Woman is *Robin Morgan* 66
The male tradition *Stephanie Markman* 67
The choosing *Liz Lochhead* 68
A working mum *Sally Flood* 70

Adman's language
Development *Robert Froman* 72
Dead news *Dai Lockwood* 73
majorca *John Cooper Clarke* 74
Early shift on the *Evening Standard* news desk
  Adrian Mitchell 75
Agatha's trousers *Helen Slavin* 76
Dusk jockey *Vernon Scannell* 77

They've got something on you
Under photographs of two party leaders, smiling *Adrian Mitchell*	78
Skinny poem *Lou Lipsitz*	79
Madam and the census man *Langston Hughes*	80
The one they took *Mary Augusta Tappage*	81
A worker's speech to a doctor *Bertolt Brecht*	82
The class game *Mary Casey*	84
Six a clock news *Tom Leonard*	85
Saw it in the papers *Adrian Mitchell*	86

Special occasions
From Lucy: carnival *James Berry*	90
Guy Fawkes *Barry Heath*	92
Removal from Glengall Grove *Carol Martin*	93
Roman holiday *Frank Collymore*	94

In work, out of work
Wages *Alan Jackson*	95
Trades *Amy Lowell*	96
A letter of application *Anita Harbottle*	97
The careers interview *Sandra Agard*	98
The production line *Bobby Pearce*	99
My dad these days *Philip Guard*	100
Let us be men *D.H. Lawrence*	101
More haste – less speed *Pamela Blackett*	102
The hangman at home *Carl Sandburg*	103

War
Green memory *Langston Hughes*	104
Madness *Robert Froman*	105
Recruited – Poplar *Margaret Postgate*	106
When my mum was a little girl *Cassandra Farquarson*	107
The chances *Wilfred Owen*	108
Casualty *Miroslav Holub*	109
Fifteen million plastic bags *Adrian Mitchell*	110
General, your tank is a powerful vehicle *Bertolt Brecht*	111
Atrocities *Siegfried Sassoon*	112

Life ending
The collier's wife   *D.H. Lawrence*   114
Death of a son   *Mary Augusta Tappage*   116
Mother to son   *Langston Hughes*   118
Note for the future   *Jim Burns*   119

Follow-up section   121

Poetry books for the classroom library   125

Index of authors   126

Acknowledgements   127

To the reader

This book is called *Speaking To You* because everything in this book is someone speaking to you.

That may seem an obvious thing to say but it isn't quite so obvious when you think that most things that are written down in books are not written with the phrases that we use when we speak to each other.

Mostly, what is written is written in a special kind of written language. If you open a history or geography book, you'll find no slang, no dialect, none of the things like 'you know' or 'I don't' or 'eh?' that we use when we speak.

And the same goes for most kinds of poetry. It's as if most poetry doesn't use our speaking voice, but it uses a special 'poetry voice' instead.

This book tries to give you the poetry of the spoken voice.

We hope it speaks to you.

Michael Rosen
David Jackson

· in the beginning was the word
in thi beginning was thi wurd
in thi beginnin was thi wurd
in thi biginnin was thi wurd
in thi biginnin wuz thi wurd
n thi biginnin wuz thi wurd
nthi biginnin wuzthi wurd
nthibiginnin wuzthiwurd
nthibiginninwuzthiwurd
· in the beginning was the sound .

Tom Leonard

Families

As soon as I could speak – I was told to listen
As soon as I could play – they taught me to work
As soon as I found a job – I married
As soon as I married – came the children
As soon as I understood them – they left me
As soon as I had learned to live – life was gone

Debbie Carnegie

Parents' sayings

You're old enough to wash your own socks.

He's not coming through this door again, I can tell you.

If it's true what your teacher said then you can say goodbye to that coat we were going to get you.

You do it and like it.

When did you last wash your feet?

Why don't you do a Saturday job?

The answer's NO.

The biscuits are for *everyone* — OK?

Don't mind me, I'm just your mother.

You haven't ridden that bike of yours for years.

You try and leave home and I'll chuck you out on your ear.

You're certainly not going to put that up on any wall in this house.

Do you know what a Hoover is?

You can pay for the next phone bill.

If you don't like this caff — find another one.

Just 'cos he's doing biology he thinks he's going to be a brain surgeon.

Do you remember that lovely Christmas when he was six?

Michael Rosen

I don't like my brother in the morning

Every morning on a Saturday and Sunday
I go to my paper round at 6.30 a.m.
and by 7.00 I am back home
and I go back to bed to get some sleep.
I make a little bit of noise
when I get into bed,
and just when I am dozing off,
my brother wakes up.
He knows I am awake
and he wants me to stay awake
so he goes outside for a pee —
I know that, because I can hear him
flush the toilet.
Then he bursts inside
and stands in front of the mirror
and says, 'SPIDER MAN!!!'

Keith Ballentine

Hugger mugger

I'd sooner be
Jumped and thumped and dumped,

I'd sooner be
Slugged and mugged . . . than *hugged* . . .

And clobbered with a slobbering
Kiss by my Auntie Jean:

You know what I mean:

Whenever she comes to stay,
You know you're bound

To get one.
A quick
  short
    peck
      would
        be
          OK.
But this is a
Whacking great
Smacking great
Wet one!

All whoosh and spit
And crunch and squeeze
And '*Dear* little boy!'
And 'Auntie's missed you!'
And 'Come to Auntie, she
Hasn't *kissed* you!'
Please don't do it, Auntie,
PLEASE!

Or if you've absolutely
Got to,

And nothing on *earth* can persuade you
Not to,

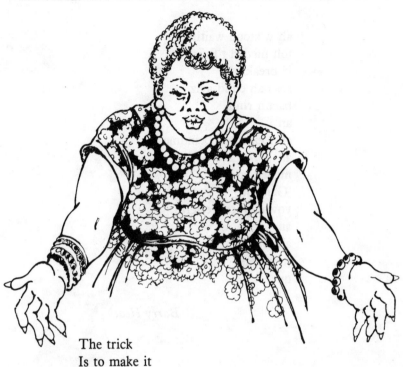

The trick
Is to make it
Quick,

You know what I mean?

For as things are,
I really would far,

Far sooner be
Jumped and thumped and dumped,

I'd sooner be
Slugged and mugged . . . than *hugged* . . .

And clobbered with a slobbering
Kiss by my Auntie

Jean!

Kit Wright

bacun rind

ah w'stood waitin
foh medad t'finish
iz breakfust
soas ah cudd ayiz
bacun rind
an
ah Lez stood beindme
an
medad sez
'Gerraht!
yowad yorn yesterdi.'
an
ah joined
tomorras
que.

Barry Heath

Mum, can I go out?

Me	Mum, can I go out?
Mum	Out where?
Me	In the village, where else?
Mum	Where in the village?
Me	I dunno – around.
Mum	Whereabouts?
Me	Just around.
Mum	Who's going to be out?
Me	Just the gang.
Mum	Who's going to be out?
Me	Just the gang.
Mum	Who's the gang?
Me	The gang's the gang, Mum.
Mum	What time will you be coming in?
Me	About 9.30.
Mum	Isn't it dark then?
Me	Yer, why?
Mum	But young girls shouldn't . . .
Me	OK Mum, you always say that. Well can I go out?
Mum	NO!!!

Helen Cranswick

The dog lovers

So they bought you
And kept you in a
Very good home
Central heating
TV
A deep freeze
A *very* good home —
No one to take you
For that lovely long run —
But otherwise
'A *very* good home'.
They fed you Pal and Chum
But not that lovely long run,
Until, mad with energy and boredom
You escaped — and ran and ran and ran
Under a car.
Today they will cry for you —
Tomorrow they will buy another dog.

Spike Milligan

School

I was walking down the stairs behind a teacher,
when I got to the bottom she came over to me and said,
'You done it.'
and I said, 'What?'
she said, 'You know what. Go on. Admit it. You did do it.'
Then she just walked off.
So I stood there trying to think what
I was meant to have done.

Sunny Caruana

First day at school

A millionbillionwillion miles from home
Waiting for the bell to go. (To go where?)
Why are they all so big, other children?
So noisy? So much at home they
must have been born in uniform
Lived all their lives in playgrounds
Spent the years inventing games
that don't let me in. Games
that are rough, that swallow you up.

And the railings.
All around, the railings.
Are they to keep out wolves and monsters?
Things that carry off and eat children?
Things you don't take sweets from?
Perhaps they're to stop us getting out
Running away from the lessins. Lessin.
What does a lessin look like?
Sounds small and slimy.
They keep them in glassrooms.
Whole rooms made out of glass. Imagine.

I wish I could remember my name
Mummy said it would come in useful.
Like wellies. When there's puddles.
Yellowwellies. I wish she was here.
I think my name is sewn on somewhere
Perhaps the teacher will read it for me.
Tea-cher. The one who makes the tea.

Roger McGough

Daydream

Pen in my hand,
questions on the board
what do I do?
Oh lord!
'What's the answer?'
I ask Tracey.
'I don't know
I was copying you!'
she replies.
The teacher, droning
on and on,
he fades,
my mind wanders
to where
Kung Fuer, kung fu's
and jumbo jets soar.
Where water flows
with blood
and sharks
devour ice cream.
Pictures melt as the
droning returns.
'What's wrong?'
teacher asks,
'nothing,'
I reply.

Deepak Kalha

School

I was born in Scarborough in Jamaica.
I didn't know my mother.
My mother leave the district when I small,
and went to St Annes.
I live with my father and my mother-in-law.

Well, I went to infants school.
I could remember I used to sleep in the class.

I left the infants school
and went to the ordinary big school.
I just wouldn't go to school.
I just feel I didn't learn anything.
When the teacher ask a question
the others put their hand up,
and I couldn't put mine up.
I wouldn't go to school any more.
I start to cry and hide from school.
I leave the home
like I go to school
and then stop on the way
and just play around on the common.

When my mother give my money
in the morning, for lunch,
I throw it away.
One of my friends told her
I wasn't going to school.
The evening I came home, she beat me.
She still send me back to the school.
I still wouldn't go.
She moved me from there.

Then she send me to Bethany school.
I wouldn't learn.
I don't know why.
I could remember one day.
Me and another boy catch a fight.
Two of his brothers came into it
and catch my pants and tear it.
Then from that day I get scared
to go back to school.
My father didn't know what was going on.
He leave home early in the morning
to work on the farm.
Come home nine o'clock.
I think his wife told him.
He say since I won't go to school,
'Go to work with me.
You going to be sorry later on.
Later on
you're going to need that read and write.'
My father take me to the farm
and I have to help he work.
I could remember one day I in the park
carrying bush.

I see my friends coming from school.
I feel so embarrassed.
I should be with them.
One of the girls said to me,
'Why didn't you come to school today?'
I didn't answer the question.
I must have been about eight.
I didn't know how to write my name.

Isaac Gordon

Conversations

Sitting in class,
listening to
conversations.
Eddy and Frog
playing cards.
'I never put that down.'
'Yes you did.'

'Shame,' says Alrick.

Kevin P. casually
beating up
Kevin B.
'Get off.'
'Shut your gob.'

Butts and Byron
doing their work.
for once.
'What about number seven.'
'Me no know.'

Tina and the two Lesleys,
talking,
'She went out last night.'
'You never believe who I saw yesterday.'

Nisha, Nayyar and Sumathi
listen to
Jackie and Claudia
arguing,
'Stop writing on my book!'
'Bloody well leave off!'

Errol points out
the window,
Dapo answers him,
'Fisk.'
'Shame.'

Tracey, Janet and Gaby
talk amongst themselves,
loudly,
'Have you done your homework?'
'Staying dinners?'

Sir stands up
'4i please be quiet!'
Mr Munro is now in
tears.

Marie and Pauline
writing,
on the desk,
'Did you see that film last night?'
'We've got French.'

Ashok and Ramji,
quiet.

Gary, Dean and Lee,
fighting,
'Stop strangling me!'
'You git.'

'I wonder why sir's got his head on the desk?'

Deepak Kalha

The class

Quite often
you sit with your back to the teacher
you bounce a ping-pong ball on the table
you practise breaking your mate's neck
you beat rhythms on his back
you sit on top of the cupboard
you climb out of the window

Sometimes
you notice there's a teacher in the room
and he or she says,
'Now I would like you to do this . . .'
Then you throw a ball of paper at the wall
you yell your mate's name three times
you break your mate's pencil up
you stick the broken pencil in your mate's ear
you throw your mate's pen in the bin
you try smacking the top of your head
    and rubbing your belly at the same time
you fall off your chair
you say,
'If frozen water is called iced water
    what do you call frozen ink?'
'Er . . iced ink?'
'Ugh. . . . YOU STINK!'
You say:
'Humpty Dumpty sat on the wall
Humpty Dumpty had a great fall
All the king's horses
and all the king's men
trod on him'

The teacher seems to be talking too.
The teacher seems to be talking to you.
The teacher says,
'I've told you what to do—so do it.'
So you say,
'What do you want us to do now sir?'

So you climb into the cupboard
you climb out of the cupboard
you jam a table into your mate's belly
you nick your mate's bag
you eat his crisps
you say, 'Get lost, earoles.'
The teacher seems to be saying to you,
'Hey. You. Sit on your own.'

So you make Match of the Day noises
you wave your arms in the air
you sing, 'Come on you re-eds'
       'Come on you re-eds'
you say, 'If you were living in a bungalow
and you painted the bedroom red,
the bathroom white,
what colour would you paint the stairs?'
'I dunno—blue?'
'No. There aren't any stairs, it's a bungalow.'
You say,
'Knock knock'
'Who's there?'
'Cows.'
'Cows who?'
'No they don't. Cows moo.'
So you bend your mate's ruler backwards
and forwards
and backwards.
It breaks.
The teacher seems to be saying to you,
'Report to the Head!'
and you say,
'Why?
That's not fair,
why pick on me,
what was I doing?'

                              Michael Rosen

Napoleon

Children, when was
Napoleon Bonaparte born,
asks teacher.

A thousand years ago, the children say.
A hundred years ago, the children say.
Last year, the children say.
No one knows.

Children, what did
Napoleon Bonaparte do,
asks teacher.

Won a war, the children say.
Lost a war, the children say.
No one knows.

Our butcher had a dog
called Napoleon,
says František.
The butcher used to beat him and the dog died
of hunger
a year ago.

And all the children are now sorry
for Napoleon.

Miroslav Holub

Proving yourself

Dumb insolence

I'm big for ten years old
Maybe that's why they get at me

Teachers, parents, cops
Always getting at me

When they get at me

I don't hit em
They can do you for that

I don't swear at em
They can do you for that

I stick my hands in my pockets
And stare at them

And while I stare at them
I think about sick

They call it dumb insolence

They don't like it
But they can't do you for it

I've been done before
They say if I get done again

They'll put me in a home
So I do dumb insolence

Adrian Mitchell

When I realised I wasn't so brave after all

Everyone had jumped the ditch on the building site.
It was about five feet wide, fifteen feet deep with wooden stakes driven into the bottom.
If I fell in I would most certainly break a few bones.
My shoes were clogged and leaden with mud.
I didn't want to jump.
The others sitting on the other side were jeering me on.
I denied being afraid.
I stood at the slippery edge of the ditch and looked down at the blunt, yellow, roughly hewn stakes
sticking up at odd angles.
The smooth wet walls of the ditch.
The wet, red, muddy ground on either side.
I took a few paces backwards and began to run.
My nerve failed me at the edge, I stopped dead almost sending myself in.
I eyed the others.
They knew I couldn't do it.

Alex Chaplin

Wall walk

THIN
WALL.
STEEP   FALL.
STEP
CARE-
FULLY
ARMS   OUT.
TIP   TIP
BUT
NOT
TOO
MUCH
TIP.
BAL-
ANCE.
AH.
     MADE IT.

Robert Froman

Delinquent

Little Julie
Has grown quite tall.
Folks say she don't like
To stay home at all.

Little Julie
Has grown quite stout.
Folks say it's not just
Stomach sticking out.

Little Julie
Has grown quite wise—
A tiger, a lion, and an owl
In her eyes.

Little Julie
Says she don't care!
What she means is:
*Nobody cares
Anywhere.*

Langston Hughes

Golden Harvest

Golden Harvest.*
The Girl Pat.
Eilan Glas.
Naturally sixteen has not much time
for all the old songs.
These two have dogged the Mod
this last afternoon, undone
the top three buttons, folded
collars open to a deep vee —
schoolgirls arm in arm
down by the harbour humming.
Arm in arm
on such high cork shoes they still
move easily
among oil and rope and smeared
rainbows of fishscales.

They giggle
or go blank
or bat back smart answers
to the young dogs (sealegs,
cuffed wellingtons) moving easily
among nets and hooks and weights.
Luminous floats,
wolf whistles.

Trouble is this town's too small.
They've twice trawled around the circuit
of mainstreet and back round church street,
sneered at every white-net Sunday hat with streamers
in the Pakistani draper's shop display.
In the autumn there's the nursing.

*Names of fishing boats in a small Scottish port.

At Woolworth's beauty counter
one smears across the back of her hand
the colour of her next kiss.
The other nets in her wiremesh self help basket
Sea Witch.
Harvest Gold.

Liz Lochhead

False friends-like

When I wer still a bwoy, an' mother's pride,
A bigger bwoy spoke up to me so kind-like,
'If you do like, I'll treat ye wi' a ride
On theäse wheel-barrow here.' Zoo I wer blind-like
To what he had a-workèn in his mind-like,
An' mounted vor a passenger inside;
An' comèn to a puddle, perty wide,
He tipp'd me in, a-grinnèn back behind-like.
Zoo when a man do come to me so thick-like,
An' sheäke my hand, where woonce he pass'd me by,
An' tell me he would do me this or that,
I can't help thinkèn o' the big bwoy's trick-like.
An' then, vor all I can but wag my hat
An' thank en, I do veel a little shy.

William Barnes

When I was 15

Ken said to me,
'You know your trouble,
you don't hold your bag right.'
'What's wrong with it?' I said.
'It's not so much the way you hold it—
It's the way you put it down.
You've got to look at it as if you hate it.
Watch me.'

He went out
he walked back in
shoulders back
elbows out
bag balanced in his hand.

'Watch me.'

He stopped walking.
His arm froze
and the bag flew out of his hand
as if he'd kicked it.
He didn't even look at it.
'Now you try,' he said.
'I'll show you where you've gone wrong.'
I went out the door,
I rambled back in again with my bag.
I stopped walking
My arm froze—just like his,
but the bag fell out of my hand
and flopped on to the floor
like a fried egg.

'Useless,' he said.
'You don't convince—that's your trouble.'
'So?' I said.
'I'm a slob. I can't change that.'

I didn't say that I *would* try and change
in case that would show I was giving in to him.
But secretly
on my own,
in my room,
in front of the mirror
I spent hours and hours
practising bag-dropping.
Walking in,
freeze the arm,
let the bag drop.
Walk in
arm freeze
bag drop.
Again and again
till I thought I had got it right.

I don't suppose any girl noticed.
I don't suppose any girl ever said to herself,
'I love the way he drops his bag . . .'

Michael Rosen

Domino

Mi enta de club, it waz quiet;
Mi start fe mek me way up de stears
Mi ear noize
Ellis, Brown, Porter an Findley play domino.

Ellis atel Findley fi rub it up
Findley atel im fe shut up;
Brown atel Findley fe play
Porter noh sae noting.

Brown warn look cool,
So im tun up im jacket collar;
Ellis tink im dread
Findley look dead
Porter shave im 'ed
Im tun barl ed.

Dem clap dun de domino
Ana mek up noize.
Dem arsk one anader if dem play yet,
Iz pass dem pass

Dema run up dem mout'
Ana shout
Six up six up
One a dem shout

De game dun now.
Soh Ellis dread, Brown cool,
Findley dead an' Porter barl'ed
Dem arl garn 'ome, garn 'ome to bed.

Rose Porter

Nooligan

I'm a nooligan
dont give a toss
in our class
I'm the boss
(well, one of them)

I'm a nooligan
got a nard 'ead
step out of line
and youre dead
(well, bleedin)

I'm a nooligan
I spray me name
all over town
footballs me game
(well, watchin)

I'm a nooligan
violence is fun
gonna be a nassassin
or a nired gun
(well, a soldier)

        Roger McGough

Letting your hair down

Reckless

Last night I was reckless
didn't brush my teeth
and went to bed tasting
my dinner all night

And it tasted good.

Pete Brown

Sittn guzzlin

sittn guzz-
lin a can
a newcastle
brown wotchn
scotsport hum-
min thi furst
movement a
nielsens thurd
symphony — happy
iz larry yi
might say;

a wuz jist turn-
in ovir thi
possibility uv
oapnin anuthir
can whin thi
centre forward
picked up
a loose baw:
hi huddiz back
tay thi
right back iz
hi caught
it wayiz in-
step n jist
faintn this way
then this
way, hi turnd
n cracked it;
jist turnd n
cracked it;
aw nwan move-
ment; in ti
thi net.

Tom Leonard

Fingerlicking

I went to the kitchen
Find de food finger licking
I tek out a de fridge
A nice big piece a chicken.
I started to nyam it
But me mammy come an grab it
And gimme a piece a licking
And sen me to me bed.

Judith Ellis

accidentally

accidentally
broke a teacup —
reminds me
how good it feels
to break things

Ishikawa Takuboku

Japanese poem translated by Carl Sesar

ee shynta ducked!

Ken Dado
an
ah Lez
wunt lemme play
an
it want fair
cos
ah ad nobody t'playwee.

an
ah picked up this'ere
building brick
an
said nah can ah play?
an
they said no
so
ah threw this'ere
building brick
an
it smashed Dado's
fruntwinda
an
ah went omm
shahtin
'Eee shunta ducked!
Ee shunt a ducked!'

Barry Heath

No swimming in the town

The swimming pool is closed —
There isn't any money.
What shall we do?
It isn't very funny.

We'll open up the school
And chase away the porter.
Turn on the taps
And fill it up with water.

Ian Serraillier

Fishermen

Hiyamac.
Lobuddy.
Binearlong?
Cuplours.
Ketchanenny?
Goddafew.
Kindarthay?
Bassencarp.
Enysizetoum?
Cuplapowns.
Hittinard?
Sordalite.
Wahchoozin?
Gobbawurms.
Fishanonaboddum?
Rydonnaboddum.
Igoddago.
Tubad.
Seeyaround.
Yeatakideezy.
Guluk.

Anon

End of a holiday

My father climbs the stairs
Above my head
And then I hear him climb
Into his bed.

Sheep bleat—the sun's last sparks
Float through the wood
Like bubbles in last week's
Old lemonade.

I wait, and then I ask
Is he all right
Up in the dark without
A proper light.

He pulls the heavy clothes
Up to his chin.
I'm fine, he says, I'm perfect.
—Goodnight, son.

Ian Hamilton Finlay

A good time

A rock concert in Belfast

Rule the Roost
Have left the stage
At long last for we want Rory.
The lights go down
A spotlight flicks on
The moment we've been waiting for.

Gerry McAvoy and Ted McKenna
Bassist and drummer of the trio
Start up the rhythm of 'Shin Kicker'
Then comes Rory
With sunburst finish battered stratocastar
Round his neck, still soundin' good.

'Brute Force and Ignorance'
Follows 'Shin Kicker'
As overhead sound to light floods on.

The hall erupts as stage is rushed
Bouncers do their job
10,000 watts of Marshal amplification versus bouncers in the
  Ulster Hall
All one can hear is 'A Souped-up Ford'.

'Moonfield' follows next—A lull in the storm
Rory breaks a string—not for long
'Too Much Alcohol' to go.

The end has come—the band leave the stage
The crowd chant 'We want Rory'
Back they come this time it's 'Hands off' and 'Fuel to the Fire'
The final encore.

Slowly the fagged audience files out feeling slightly battered
  but exhilarated
Out onto the cold dreary street—Bedford Street Belfast.
Policemen lean against Land Rovers eating hamburgers
Guns propped under their arms
Distant radio crackle audible
Sounding not a bit like Rory's lead runs
Walking into Donegall Square a saracen followed by a pig
  hurtled by
Blaring music of another kind.
A bomb goes off somewhere in the city
We're back to 20th century civilisation.

Patrick Gibson

Two Rastaman

Two Rasta jus a stepit in a Brixton hall
  wid dem hat stan tall, red gol and green
                              but them still rankin you know
                                    dem jus come fe lisan
  to de sweet musical beat of fat man
  dem jus come fe step it
                              nobody trouble dem
                              no body look pan dem
  nobody mess wid dem fe dey will cut you down
                              dem jus a smoke up dem cally
                              dem jus a wine up a dolly
dem jus a rankin

Michael Payne

Dub rock

Heavy, heavy,
  hard rock-up dub
    strong
Trenchtown dread getting hip with the bass,
Tearing up his mind
    strong
Heavy Trenchtown rock,
  dub dub dub
  drum and bass
  drum and bass
Riddim licking his mind,
Searching his soul,
Breakin' down his barriers
Erected to hide him.
Locks falling to shoulders,
Jah on his mind.
  lick it back
  heavy tune
  what a bass
  what a beat
Linking him to the past.
Oh Africa — Land of the roaming Lion,
Ras — Conquering Lion of the Tribe of Judah.
  celestial dub
  high bass-line riff
  strong drum beat
Pounding his soul
Like a cool breeze cutting through the high grass,
Parting them
Leaving no secret hidden
  heavy bass line
  strong drum beat
Searching, searching,
Hard Trenchtown dub rock
  yeah

Hugh Boatswain

Blues for Stevie Wonder

I wish I could know
what Stevie know.
I wish I could blow
like Stevie blow.
I wish I could see
what Stevie see.
I wish I could be
what Stevie be,
an the Wonder
of Stevie Wonder be.
I can know
what Stevie know,
an I can blow what
Stevie blow,
an I can see what
Stevie see, cause
Stevie Wonder,
  He be me!

Sam Greenlee

Race

Questionnaired

'Tell me again—the name of your wife,
her age both now and when you were married,
children—alive, dead or miscarried,
the name of her father and your mother,
everyone's sister and anyone's brother;

What did you say was the name of your wife?
Is she the second or was she the first?
Did she speak what had been rehearsed?

Income tax—how many dependants?
We'll have to make a few amendments
to previous statements now denied . . .
Did you declare what you couldn't hide?

By the way, what's the name of your wife?

Is this your present or previous life?'

'Sir, I have told you, I tell you once more—
I still have the one wife I had before.
It's not a question of reincarnation,
simply a matter of immigration.
Dream or nightmare, this is my life
as I mouth
      the sounds
           of the name
                of my wife.'

Tessa Stiven

Immigrants

The chief change
I've noted
among
White Folks is
now they talkin
bout us in code.
Like,
Stateside when they
say:
crime in the streets or
welfare cheats
they talkin bout us.
An in Britain
when they say
Immigrants, guess
who they mean?
I mean, they got
Cypriots, Pakistanis,
Indians, Spanish an
Italians,
but, even if yo
Great-great-great-great
Grandaddy was the
Dude turned on Ol Will
in a stable an
caused him to write
Othello, you still
an Immigrant if yo
skin is other than
fish-belly white.
Quite!
Maybe it takes as
long to become
A Black Briton
as it does to grow
them Midlands lawns

nobody but birds
walk on.
That would be cool
if they laid the
same standards on
everybody else come
here since the
Norman Invasion.
Like,
how bout that
German Lady layin
up in Buckingham Palace?
I mean,
how come the Queen
ain't un
Immu-grunt?

Sam Greenlee

Ballad of the landlord

Landlord, landlord,
My roof has sprung a leak
Don't you 'member I told you about it
Way last week?

Landlord, landlord,
These steps is broken down.
When you come up yourself
It's a wonder you don't fall down.

Ten Bucks you say I owe you?
Ten Bucks you say is due?
Well, that's Ten Bucks more'n I'll pay you
Till you fix this house up new.

What? You gonna get eviction orders?
You gonna cut off my heat?
You gonna take my furniture and
Throw it in the street?

Um-huh! You talking high and mighty.
Talk on—till you get through.
You ain't gonna be able to say a word
If I land my fist on you.

Police! Police!
Come and get this man!
He's trying to ruin the government
And overturn the land!

Copper's whistle!
Patrol bell!
Arrest.

Precinct Station.
Iron cell.
Headlines in press:

MAN THREATENS LANDLORD

TENANT HELD NO BAIL

JUDGE GIVES NEGRO 90 DAYS IN COUNTY JAIL

Langston Hughes

Harassment

One evenin, me a com from wok,
An a run fe ketch de bus,
Two police start fe run me dung,
Jus fe show how me no hav no luck,
Dem ketch me and start to mek a fus
Sas, a long time dem a watch how me
A heng, heng, round de shop

Me say me? What? Heng round shop?
From morning me daa wok,
Me only jus stop,
An if onoo tink a lie me a tell,
Gwaan go ask de Manager.

Dem insisted I was a potential thief,
And teck me to de station,
Anyway, dem sen and call me relations,
Wen dem com it was a big relief,
Fe se som one me own colour,
At least, who would talk and laugh wid me,

An me still lock up in a Jail,
So till me people dem insist that
Dem go a me wok to get som proof,
The police man dem nearly hit the roof,
Becaus dem feel dem was so sure,
That is me dem did have dem eyes on
Boy, I don't know what's rong
With these babylon men,
But dem can't tell one black man,
From de other one,

Anyway, when me reach me wok place,
Straight away de manager recognize me face,
And we go check me card,
Fe se sa me dis clock out

So me gather strength and say to de coppers,
Leggo me, onoo don't know wey onoo on about,
You want fe se dem face sa dem a apologize,
But wen me look pon how me nearly face disgrace,
It mek me want fe kus and fight,

But wey de need, in a babylon sight,
If yu right yu rong,
And wen yu rong you double rong,

So me a beg onoo, teck heed
Always have a good alibi,
Because even though yu innocent
Someone always a try
Fe mek yu bid freedom goodbye.

Frederick Williams

The 100 Centre Street, boy, you better dress up neat blues

You speak English
Yes Sir
Speak up, I can't hear you—
   You speak English
Yes Sir
Can you afford a lawyer
No Sir
OK. Legal Aid.
   Put him in
Next case

Stand up straight and take your hands
   out of your pocket
Yes Sir
Where's your family? Why isn't your family here?
My mother works
What's that? Speak up.
My mother works
Well doesn't she know that you're in
   serious trouble? We all work
   but doesn't she know she has an
   obligation to this court to be here?
Yes Sir
Well you can just wait. You go back and wait
   and we'll give your mother time to come
   Call the case later
But my mother's at work
Call the next case.

What is this? A sentence?
Yes your Honour
Any motions?
No your Honour. I'd just like to say the boy
   does have a job and this is his first offence
Shoplifting is theft Mr Defense Attorney, are you
   aware of that
Yes Sir
Six months in the city prison
Call the next case.

Anon

He and she

First kiss

Suddenly;
(after nearly an hour of fidgeting about
on the cold manky steps of her flats
—and she really did have to go in you know—)

our cracked lips rustled
and I had my first taste of her chewing-gum-mouth.

Adam Pritchard

Would you believe it

— Jacky's going out with Peter —
— Which one? NOT the one with spots —
— No of course not, Peter DAVIS —
— Don't believe you
        how d'you know? —
— Tracy told me but you mustn't say
I said so —
        — course not
how did she find out? —
— Well,
Phillipa, that's Tracy's mate the one in 3G
her mate Mandy's sister Carol's
best friend Susan and her boyfriend
(his name's Peter)
saw them
        Coming Out The Pictures

—(But you mustn't tell A SOUL
'cos Jacky's also going out
with someone else as well . . .)

Mick Gowar

When we met I said, 'Where shall we go?'
She said, 'I don't mind.'
I said, 'I don't mind either. Anywhere you like.'
She said, 'I don't know really. What do you think?'
I said, 'I don't know.'
She said, 'You say.'
So I said, 'Want to walk?'
So she said, 'Where to?'
So I said, 'I don't know.'
So she said, 'A walk? There's no point in just walking.'
So I said, 'No I suppose not. Shall we just stay here then?'
Then she said, 'No. There's no point in going nowhere.'
So I said, 'Well where shall we go?'
And she said, 'I don't mind . . . .'

Michael Rosen

he and she

she	it's the same thing
he	no it is not
she	yes it is
he	let's not go through all that again
she	right
he	why do you always have the last word?
she	you have it
he	thank you
	(*pause*)
she	don't mention it
he	why can't you shut up
she	why can't *you* shut up
he	shut up
she	you shut up
	(*both together*)
he ⎱	shut up
she ⎰	shut up

R. D. Laing

The role of women

Advert

You start by sinking into his arms
  and you end up with
your arms in his sink.

Anon

Poem for my sister

My little sister likes to try my shoes,
to strut in them,
admire her spindle-thin twelve-year-old legs
in this season's styles.
She says they fit her perfectly,
but wobbles
on their high heels, they're
hard to balance.

I like to watch my little sister
playing hopscotch, admire the neat hops-and-skips of her,
their quick peck,
never-missing their mark, not
over-stepping the line.
She is competent at peever.

I try to warn my little sister
about unsuitable shoes,
point out my own distorted feet, the callouses,
odd patches of hard skin.
I should not like to see her
in my shoes.
I wish she could stay
sure footed,
       sensibly shod.

Liz Lochhead

Let us now praise fearful men

Let us now praise fearful men

the man who thinks twice before
he frames his words
the man who is afraid to let his eyes
wander
too freely
the man who holds back
from opening doors
leaping to pay your bill
buy your drink
let us now praise fearful men

Let us now praise fearful men

they still nurse
past bruises
they anticipate more to come
they have been attacked
abandoned
neglected
rejected
done without
positively NOT NEEDED
let us now praise fearful men

Michelene Wandor

Woman is

— kicking strongly in your mother's womb, upon which she is told, 'It must be a boy, if it's so active!'

— being tagged with a *pink* beaded bracelet thirty seconds after you are born, and wrapped in *pink* blankets five minutes thereafter.

— being labelled a tomboy when all you wanted to do was climb that tree and look out and see a distance.

— learning to sit with your legs crossed, even when your feet can't touch the floor yet.

— hating boys—because they're allowed to do things you want to do but are forbidden to—and being told hating boys is a phase.

— wondering why your father gets mad now and then, but your mother mostly sighs a lot.

— seeing grown-ups chuckle when you say you want to be an engineer or doctor when you grow up—learning to say you want to be a mommy or a nurse, instead.

— feeling basically comfortable in your own body, but gradually learning to hate it because you are: too short or tall, too fat or thin, thick-thighed or big-wristed, large-eared or stringy-haired, short-necked or long-armed, bowlegged, knock-kneed or pigeon-toed—*something* that *might* make boys not like you.

— wanting to kill yourself because of pimples, dandruff, or a natural tendency to sweat—and discovering that commercials about miracle products just lie.

— having your first real human talk with your mother and being told about all her old hopes and lost ambitions, and how you can't fight it, and that's just the way it is: life, sex, men, the works—and loving her and hating her for having been so beaten down.

— having your first real human talk with your father and being told about all *his* old hopes and lost ambitions, and how women really have it easier, and 'what a man really wants in a woman,'—and loving him and hating him for having been beaten down—and for beating down your mother in turn.

— coming home from work—and starting *in* to work: unpack the groceries, fix supper, wash up the dishes, rinse out some laundry etc., etc.

— feeling a need to say 'thank you' when your guy actually fixes *himself* a meal now that you're dying with the flu.

Robin Morgan

the male tradition

standing-up-and-fighting-like-a-man is a good deal easier than sitting down and writing like a woman.

Stephanie Markman

The choosing

We were first equal Mary and I
with the same coloured ribbons in mouse-coloured hair,
and with equal shyness
we curtseyed to the lady councillor
for copies of Collins' Children's Classics.
First equal, equally proud.

Best friends too Mary and I
a common bond in being cleverest (equal)
in our small school's small class.
I remember
the competition for top desk
or to read aloud the lesson
at school service.
And my terrible fear
of her superiority at sums.

I remember the housing scheme
Where we both stayed.
The same house, different homes,
where the choices were made.

I don't know exactly why they moved,
but anyway they went.
Something about a three-apartment
and a cheaper rent.
But from the top deck of the high-school bus
I'd glimpse among the others on the corner
Mary's father, mufflered, contrasting strangely
with the elegant greyhounds by his side.
He didn't believe in high-school education,
especially for girls,
or in forking out for uniforms.

Ten years later on a Saturday —
I am coming home from the library —
sitting near me on the bus,
Mary
with a husband who is tall,
curly haired, has eyes
for no one else but Mary.
Her arms are round the full-shaped vase
that is her body.
Oh, you can see where the attraction lies
in Mary's life —
not that I envy her, really.

And I am coming from the library
with my arms full of books.
I think of the prizes that were ours for the taking
and wonder when the choices got made
we don't remember making.

Liz Lochhead

A working mum

From morning, till night,
Life is one maddening rush.
The alarm bell rings,
You awake to a fuss.
Jump from your bed, to fight,
For a place on the bus.
Someone, who had stood
Close behind you,
Now you discover
Is in front of the queue.

You don't want trouble.
So what do you do?
You stand there fuming,
The bus draws alongside,
A quick kick on her heel
Now you're climbing inside.
You smile at the conductor,
It's just made your day,
She's still looking around her
While the bus draws away.

You arrive in work
At the stroke of nine,
You clock your card
The weather is fine.
You smile all around,
'Good Morning' to you.
Then a voice in your ear
Bawls, 'Have you nothing to do?'
You sit down quickly,
You have laddered your tights.

Seems today you have
Nothing but frights.
You keep your head down,
You daren't look up.
The hooter blows,
You run for a cup.
The canteen is full,
Back in the queue.
You wait so long,
The hooter's just blew.

Though you feel thirsty
You have to get back,
If you dawdle too long
You will get the sack.
So you rush and you pant
Till you get through the day.
There goes the hooter,
You're now on your way.
You join the bus queue,
The one at the top.

The bus is full,
It won't even stop
You are hungry and cold,
You've had a long day.
No wonder your hair
Shows streaks of grey.
You have made it at last,
There is the gate.
Time for a cuppa?
'Mum, why are you late?'

Sally Flood

Adman's language

Development

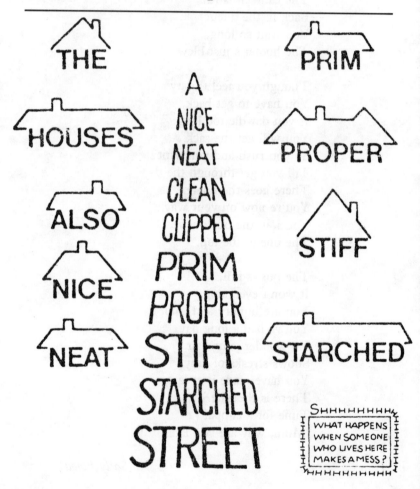

Robert Froman

Dead news

Three lines
third page.
One paragraph
in the corner.
Woman raped,
girl attacked.
Not really news,
but it fills in space.

BOLD LETTERS
FRONT PAGE.
Latest edition!
News at Ten.
RIPPER STRIKES AGAIN
WOMAN BRUTALLY MURDERED
and SEXUALLY ASSAULTED!

Only dead women
make the headlines.

Dai Lockwood

majorca

fasten your seat belts says the voice
inside the plane you can hear no noise
engines made by rolls-royce
take your choice
make mine majorca

check out the parachutes can't be found
alert the passengers they'll be drowned
a friendly mug says settle down
when i come round i'm gagged and bound
for majorca

here comes the neat hostess
and her unapproachable flip finesse
i found the meaning of the word excess
they've got little bags if you want to make a mess
i fancied cuba but it cost a lot less
to majorca
(whose blonde sand fondly kisses the cool fathoms
of the blue mediterranean)

they packed us into the white hotel
you could still smell the polycell
and the white paint in the air-conditioned cells
the waiter smells of fake chanel
gauloises garlic as well
said if i like i could call him miguel
well really

i got drunk with another fella
who'd just brought up a previous paella
wanted a fight but said they were yella
in majorca

the guitars rang the castinets clicked
the dancers stamped the dancers kicked
the double diamond flowed like sick
mother's pride tortilla and chips
pneumatic drills you can't kip
take a dip you're in the shit
if you sing in the street you're knicked
in majorca

the heat made me sick i had to stay in the shade
must have been something in the lemonade
but by the balls of franco i paid
i had to pawn my bucket and spade
next year i take the international brigade
to majorca

John Cooper Clarke

Early shift on the Evening Standard *news desk*

Fog Chaos Grips South

A thick blanket of fog lay across Southern England this morning like a thick blanket—

'Don't let's call it a thick blanket today Joe, let's call it a sodden yellow eiderdown.'

'Are you insane?'

Adrian Mitchell

Agatha's trousers

When Agatha arrives in her
  yellow trousers,
The ones that make her legs look
  like overripe bananas,
They all say,
'You look fantastic,'
'So trendy.'
When I'm with them I say,
'You look really smart, I must get
  a pair just the same,'
But when I'm alone I think,
'I mustn't get a pair like that,'
Because I know that if I did
They'd all say,
'You look fantastic,'
'So trendy,'
But they'd all be thinking
  that my legs look like
  overripe bananas.

Helen Slavin

Dusk jockey

'Good evening, everyone.
Let me remind you who I am.
I am not your favourite man.
You've never seen me but you know my voice.
The tunes I play make none of you rejoice:
They're what you'd call decidedly unpop.
The only charts that they'd be sure to top
Would be a list of sounds you most detest.
Now and then I bring along a guest
To give my programme added interest:
I had a vampire in the studio
No longer than a half-an-hour ago
But he was thirsty and he had to go.
He says he hopes he'll visit some of you
For one quick drink before the night is through.
If you're anaemic you can sleep quite tight
Except a news flash filtered through last night:
A madman has infected all supplies
Of water everywhere. Perhaps all lies,
But I wouldn't bet on it if I were you.
And now a card from Mr Pettigrew
Who says he's looking forward keenly to
The funeral of Mrs Pettigrew.
Some music now for Mrs Thumb and Tom—
The Zombies' March and Lepers' Chorus from
An opera whose title slips my mind.
And then I've got to go, before the blind
Of total night comes down. But don't believe I'm through:
Dusk is the time I find most work to do.
I've got to groom my mount while there's still light;
I'll ride my mare into your sleep tonight.

Vernon Scannell

They've got something on you

Under photographs of two party leaders, smiling

These two smiled so the photographer
Could record their smiles
FOR YOU

As they smiled these smiles
They were thinking all the time
OF YOU

They smile on the rich
They smile on the poor
They smile on the victim in his village
They smile on the killer in his cockpit

Yes, Mummy and Daddy
Are smiling, smiling
AT YOU

please try to smile back.

Adrian Mitchell

Skinny poem

Skinny
poem,
all
your
ribs
showing
even
without
a
deep
breath

thin
legs
rotted
with
disease.

Live
here!
on
this
page,
barely
making
it,
like
the
mass
of
mankind.

Lou Lipsitz

Madam and the census man

The census man,
The day he came round,
Wanted my name
To put it down.

I said, JOHNSON,
ALBERTA K.
But he hated to write
The K that way.

He said, What
Does K stand for?
I said, K—
And nothing more.

he said, I'm gonna put it
K—A—Y.
I said, If you do,
You lie.

My mother christened me
ALBERTA K.
You leave my name
Just that way!

He said, Mrs,
(With a snort)
Just a K
Makes your name too short.

I said, I don't
Give a damn!
Leave me and my name
Just like I am!

Furthermore, rub out
That MRS, too—
I'll have you know
I'm *Madam* to you!

Langston Hughes

The one they took

They took one on me, the Welfare did.
They put him out at Horsefly.
You see, this one I had was a likeable little fellow,
but he started taking fits.

Well, that woman came for him.
In a way I was kind of sorry
and I was kind of mad at that woman too.
I hated her, I told her,
'What makes you so important now?
Why now to be so important?
The minute I raise him
you come taking him away!'

I didn't want him to go.
But I guess she had orders from people.
You know how everything goes
in these government offices.

I guess I loved him,
that little fellow.

Mary Augusta Tappage

A worker's speech to a doctor

We know what makes us ill.
When we are ill we are told
That it's you who will heal us.

For ten years, we are told
You learned healing in fine schools
Built at the people's expense
And to get your knowledge
Spent a fortune.
So you must be able to heal.

Are you able to heal?

When we come to you
Our rags are torn off us
And you listen all over our naked body.
As to the cause of our illness
One glance at our rags would
Tell you more. It is the same cause that wears out
Our bodies and our clothes.

The pain in our shoulder comes
You say, from the damp; and this is also the reason
For the stain on the wall of our flat.
So tell us:
Where does the damp come from?

Too much work and too little food
Make us feeble and thin.
Your prescription says:
Put on more weight.
You might as well tell a bullrush
Not to get wet.

How much time can you give us?
We see: one carpet in your flat costs
The fees you earn from
Five thousand consultations.

You'll no doubt say
You are innocent. The damp patch
On the wall of our flats
Tells the same story.

Bertolt Brecht

The class game

How can you tell what class I'm from?
I can talk posh like some
With an 'Olly in me mouth
Down me nose, wear an 'at not a scarf
With me second-hand clothes.
So why do you always wince when you hear
Me say 'Tara' to me 'Ma' instead of 'Bye Mummy dear'?
How can you tell what class I'm from?
'Cos we live in a corpy, not like some
In a pretty little semi, out Wirral way
And commute into Liverpool by train each day?
Or did I drop my unemployment card
Sitting on your patio (We have a yard)?
How can you tell what class I'm from?
Have I a label on me head, and another on me bum?
Or is it because my hands are stained with toil
Instead of soft lily-white with perfume and oil?
Don't I crook me little finger when I drink me tea
Say toilet instead of bog when I want to pee?
Why do you care what class I'm from?
Does it stick in your gullet like a sour plum?
Well, mate! A cleaner is me mother
   A docker is me brother
   Bread pudding is wet nelly
   And me stomach is me belly
And I'm proud of the class that I come from.

Mary Casey

Six a clock news

this is thi
six a clock
news thi
man said n
thi reason
a talk wia
BBC accent
iz coz yi
widny wahnt
mi ti talk
aboot thi
trooth wia
voice lik
wanna yoo
scruff. if
a toktaboot
thi trooth
lik wanna yoo
scruff yi
widny thingk
it wuz troo.
jist wanna yoo
scruff tokn.
thirza right
way ti spell
ana right way
ti tok it. this
is me tokn yir
right way a
spellin. this
is ma trooth.
yooz doant no
thi trooth
yirsellz cawz
yi canny talk
right. this is
the six a clock
nyooz. belt up.

Tom Leonard

Saw it in the papers

I will not say her name
Because I believe she hates her name.

But there was this woman who lived in Yorkshire.

Her baby was two years old.
She left him, strapped in his pram, in the kitchen.
She went out.
She stayed with friends.
She went out drinking.

The baby was hungry.
Nobody came.
The baby cried.
Nobody came.
The baby tore at the upholstery of his pram.
Nobody came.

She told the police:
'I thought the neighbours would hear him crying,
and report it to someone who would come
and take him away.'

Nobody came.

The baby died of hunger.

She said she'd arranged for a girl,
Whose name she couldn't remember,
To come and look after the baby
While she stayed with friends.
Nobody saw the girl.
Nobody came.

Her lawyer said there was no evidence
of mental instability.
But the man who promised to marry her
Went off with another woman.

And when he went off, this mother changed
from a mother who cared for her two-year-old baby
into a mother who did not seem to care at all.
There was no evidence of mental instability.

The Welfare Department spokesman said:
'I do not know of any plans for an inquiry.
We never became deeply involved.'
Nobody came.
There was no evidence of mental instability.

When she was given love
She gave love freely to her baby.
When love was torn away from her
she locked her love away.
It seemed that no one cared for her.
She seemed to stop caring.
Nobody came.
There was no evidence of mental instability.

Only love can unlock locked-up-love.

Manslaughter: She pleaded Guilty.
She was sentenced to be locked up
In prison for four years.

Is there any love in prisons?

She must have been in great pain.

Now she is locked up.
There is love in prisons,
But it is all locked up.

What she did to him was terrible.
There was no evidence of mental instability.
What we are doing to her is terrible.
There is no evidence of mental instability.

Millions of children starve, but not in England.
What we do not do for them is terrible.

Is England's love locked up in England?
There is no evidence of mental instability.

Only love can unlock locked-up love.

When I read about it in the papers I cried.
When my friend read about it in the papers he cried.
We shared our tears.
They did not help her at all.

She has been locked up
For locking up her love.
There was no evidence of mental instability.

Unlock all of your love.
You have enough to feed all those millions of children.
Unlock all of your love.
You have enough for this woman.

Cry if you like.
Do something if you can. You can.

Unlock your love and send it to this woman.
I am sending her my love.

Adrian Mitchell

Special occasions

From Lucy: carnival

Mi dear, yesterday I did go Carnival
or Mas, as the Trinnies call it.
Mas comes from Masquerade, you know.
But Jamaica Masquerade is pickney
party, compared to royalty occasion.
Mi dear, this elaborates big big.

A whole London district in
street jumpup, in costumes,
in ordinary clothes, even barefoot.
A dozen costume ban's, floats galore
like stars. Should see kaftans an' gowns.

An' if masquerader not priest
he a witch, if he not satan
he a fairy, if he not Red Indian
he a jumby beas'*, among
countless shapes movin' strong colour.

An' in sunshine, in Jubilee
Carnival, in the drummin'
an' the steelin', in
the mix' crowd revellin',
come the violence an' the panic.

Black youths charge, mi dear.
So the swings of sticks
an' stones an' slashes. An'
a black face comes up on TV
talkin' again 'bout violence—
'bout problems all the time.

*jumby beas': a ghost

An' us together, Sue, mi Trinidad
frien', who did sweeten up
all mornin', to have han's of rings
roun' seethrough dress, an' her man
with pretty shirt open down, an'
fe mi dear one, we did sidown
in the car. We eat rotis an' patties.
We drink rum punch, mi dear.

An' now day later, we have
not'n' lef', as real woman, real
man. We jus' know we dead. But Leela,
don' everyone of we at heart
is peacock an' satan an' angel?

It true true, 'A clever man who
drives 'way hunger
jus' workin' up his jaws'.

James Berry

Guy Fawkes

we wantud best Guy Fawkes
on ower street
so widressed ower lez
up
wipurra stick upiz back
a stick up each sleeve
one up each trahser
leg
an purrim in a barra

along Crown street
up Richo an dahn
Big Barn Lane,
thed neva seen owt
like it
rait prahd wewus
weus pockets jinglin
an lez stiff as a
cork

wistopped ahtside this
misers ahhs an ah
knocked ont doower
'Penny fut guy mista!'
ah shahtud t'misruble
sod
an ee cum aht wavin
a big axe an ah
run

Lez cuddunt run cos
ee warrin barra
so wileft im
'ah'll geeya blewdy
guy' shahtud miser
an went t'chop it up

un lez jumped aht
fraitenin miser t'
death

miser dropt axe
anrun up path
an ower lez run
stiffleggud dahnt
lane shahtin 'Wayit
f'me! Wayit f'me!'

Barry Heath

Removal from Glengall Grove

All the neighbours peering out of their windows
Trying to see who's going.
Along comes the great lorry
In goes settee, chair and tables, chairs.
Little nick nacks off the wall.
Out comes flower pots plants an all.
All the kids are pestering the driver
'What ya doing Mister, who's is that?'
Everybody comes out of their doors.
Mainly to see what you've got
And what they haven't.

Carol Martin

Roman holiday

O, It was a lovely funeral!
  One hundred and thirty-two cars,
And three of them packed high with flowers
And the streets thronged with people—
It reminded me of the Coronation—
And then such a beautiful service:
Organ and full choir of course,
And hardly a dry eye in the chapel.
And there were so many people present that they all couldn't
    get in and ever so many of them had to stand outside
    and during the service there was such a hard shower,
And most of the gentlemen in morning coats and top hats too.
And a well-dressed respectable-looking woman turned to me
And asked me—
Poor creature, she could scarcely articulate the words—
If it was true he'd really died from what we heard,
And I told her it was only too true, poor man.
And it wasn't until afterwards that I discovered
It really wasn't *his* funeral at all.
Because there was another one that evening and they had both
    got mixed up in all the confusion;
And I do think they ought to see to it that better
    arrangements should be made—
I mean, it can put one out so;
And when I did manage to get outside and reach the grave
It was all over.
But it really was a lovely funeral,
And I don't know when I've cried so much.
And that reminds me, my dear:
Have you heard that his youngest daughter
Has run away
With the chauffeur?

Frank Collymore

In work, out of work

Wages

every week
   afore we goes galumphin intae the office
to get wir pey
   ma mate Bob leaves his bunnet
ootside on the radiator
'whit fer' A says 'aw ye ken' says Bob
   'A aye tak ma hat off
     in the presence o money'

Alan Jackson

Trades

I want to be a carpenter,
To work all day long in clean wood,
Shaving it into little thin slivers
Which screw up into curls behind my plane;
Pounding square, black nails into white boards,
With the claws of my hammer glistening
Like the tongue of a snake.
I want to shingle a house,
Sitting on the ridge pole in a bright breeze.
I want to put the shingles on neatly,
Taking great care that each is directly between two
  others.
I want my hands to have the tang of wood:
Spruce, Cedar, Cypress.
I want to draw a line on a board with a flat pencil,
And then saw along that line,
With the sweet-smelling sawdust piling up in a
  yellow heap at my feet.
That is the life!
Heigh-ho!
It is much easier than to write this poem.

Amy Lowell

A letter of application

Dear Sir,
(de dah, de dah).
I am seeking employment,
(de dah).
I admire your organization
(do I hell)
And I hope that you can offer me
A post.
I write shorthand at one-twenty
And type at fifty—words per minute.
I keep books,
Have (reasonable) looks,
Can supply reference
A dozen certificates
And the fixed charming smile
Of a robot.

At the end of it all,
What shall I get?
A little brown packet
With which to console
A lost identity—
A breaking heart.

Anita Harbottle

The careers interview

You sit outside in a draughty corridor
For what seems like hours.
Finally, you are summoned.
Entering, you see two people sitting at a desk,
Smiling.
What the hell have they to laugh at?
They begin to talk about your 'career'.
You sit and smile, pretend to be listening.
'Why are you taking that lesson again
When you already have an O Level?'
She means my C.S.E. Grade One.
Big Deal.
Not everyone considers that an O Level pass.
She sits there, tells me off.
She says I've done nothing towards my career.
She thinks she knows everything.
Anytime I go to my so-called careers teacher
He has nothing to give me.
So I have to do everything by myself.
And everyone is NOT very helpful.
Naturally he doesn't say that.
I'm really fed up.
I feel like shouting at them.
They feel they are being ever so damn nice,
But how can you change a person's life in fifteen minutes?
They seem to think it can be done.
I am angry with the whole thing.
Maybe I am wrong to be angry,
But I am.
There is no one I can talk it over with.

At last it is finished.
I leave the room
Making up my mind never to return.

Sandra Agard

The production line

Nick paints the outside
Stan paints the inside
They do it all through the day
Tom does the nuts up
Bill does the bolts up
They always do it that way
Alf puts the wheels on
Bert puts the tyres on
They fix 'em so they're O.K.
Ted puts the engine
Arthur puts the boot in
But Fred's ill and he's not here today
Len puts the front seat in
George puts the back seat in
They fix 'em so they'll stay
Dan puts the lights on
Henry puts the bumpers on
Waiting for a tea break so they can get away
John puts the steering wheels in
Charlie puts the key in
And drives the car away
They can't stop long
Because as soon as that one's gone
There's another one on the way.

Bobby Pearce

my dad these days

my dad takes me down the post office
the day his giro comes
to get me out from under mums feet he says
but i know he likes me to go with him

he smokes a lot in the queue
stands hunchy like hes thinking
like when him and mum
have had a barney
and hes not going to be
the next one to say nothing

when they give him the lolly
he jerks his shoulders
like as if hes glad to get it
but still he dont like taking it

on the way home he gives me a piggyback
gallops and makes a noise like a donkey
till he gets puffed

he gets more laughy
soon as hes out the post office
he buys some fags before we get indoors
and i get a mars bar or what i like

then he gives mum most of the lolly
and she rolls her eyes up
like saying strike me is this all

dad sits hunchy more than he done
when he was up the factory
he coughs a lot and mum says
what you expect like a flaming chimney you are

then they have a barney about that

i like going down the post office with dad
but he was more laughy
when he was up the factory

Philip Guard

Let us be men

For God's sake, let us be men
not monkeys minding machines
or sitting with our tails curled
while the machine amuses us, the radio or film or
　gramophone.

Monkeys with a bland grin on our faces.

D. H. Lawrence

More haste—less speed

Press of the plunger; clatter of the coals;
The shotfirer's fist went down.

The dust clouds smothered and swarmed the space
When the roofs and 'chocks' battered through;
The pitman dashed and darted to the 'kist',
But one Putter was kept back, alone.

'Ah hinney, dinnit cry, a'thou' he was yer man
An' slogged for you an' the bairns.
An Mate, dinnit mourn, a'thou' he was yer marra
An' shared yer watter and bait.

Tucker he couldn't crawl along the face
An' died wi stench on his chest;
Jinnie was left with fowerteen bairns
—An' not a shillin' behint 'er.

'Jinnie dinnit sob, Jinnie dinnit bubble
You've still got yer compen.,
Mak 'em some puddings an' stotty cyaikes
An' fill 'em up wi' broth!'

The dreary seam of 'black nuggets',
A Putter's job left empty;
Choked because of his Deputy's impatience
To signal the coals to fall.

Pamela Blackett

The hangman at home

What does the hangman think about
When he goes home at night from work?
When he sits down with his wife and
Children for a cup of coffee and a
Plate of ham and eggs, do they ask
Him if it was a good day's work
And everything went well or do they
Stay off some topics and talk about
The weather, baseball, politics
And the comic strips in the papers
And the movies? Do they look at his
Hands when he reaches for the coffee
Or the ham and eggs? If the little
Ones say, Daddy, play horse, here's
A rope—does he answer like a joke:
I seen enough rope for today?
Or does his face light up like a
Bonfire of joy and does he say:
It's a good and dandy world we live
In. And if a white face moon looks
In through a window where a baby girl
Sleeps and the moon-gleams mix with
Baby ears and baby hair—the hangman—
How does he act then? It must be easy
For him. Anything is easy for a hangman,
I guess.

Carl Sandburg

War

Green memory

A wonderful time—the War:
when money rolled in
and blood rolled out.
    But blood
    was far away
    from here—
Money was near.

Langston Hughes

Madness

I'M 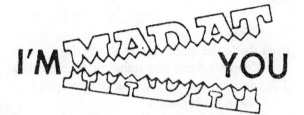 YOU

YOU'RE 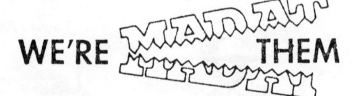 ME

WE'RE  THEM

SNAP!

Robert Froman

Recruited — Poplar

March, 1917

>*They say — they say*

(And that's the bugles going all the day
Past Cooper's Arms and round by Stepney way
Till you'll be mad for hearing of them play)
>*They — they say*

You were the finest stuff men ever had
To make into a soldier. And they say
They put the needed strength and spirit in you,
Straightened your shoulders made you clean and true,
And fit for England's service — I can say
They clothed you warm and fed and worked you fair
The first time in your life, on Derby Day;
Maybe that did a little — Anyway
They made a man out of you this year, the sort
That England's rich and proud to own, they say
>*They say — they say*

And so they went and killed you. That's their way.

Margaret Postgate

When my mum was a little girl
In France during the war,
   she says,
Every morning
She had to cycle past the
   town-hall
On her way to school
Every morning
She had to cycle past the
   town-hall,
Where sometimes they took
   people at night,
Past the thick grey boots of
   the men who stood there,
She never saw their faces,
   she says,
And every morning
She had to cycle past those
Thick grey boots planted
   wide apart.
And every morning
She heard the screams
As she cycled past the town-hall
On her way to school.

Cassandra Farquarson

The chances

I mind as 'ow the night afore that show
Us five got talkin',—we was in the know.
'Over the top to-morrer; boys, we're for it.
First wave we are, first ruddy wave; that's tore it!'
'Ah well,' says Jimmy,—an' 'e's seen some scrappin' –
'There ain't no more nor five things as can 'appen:
Ye get knocked out; else wounded—bad or cushy;
Scuppered; or nowt except yer feelin' mushy.'

One of us got the knock-out, blown to chops.
T'other was 'urt, like, losin' both 'is props.
An' one, to use the word of 'ypocrites,
'Ad the misfortoon to be took be Fritz.
Now me, I wasn't scratched, praise God Amighty,
(Though next time please I'll thank 'im for a blighty).
But poor young Jim, 'e's livin' an' 'e's not;
'E reckoned 'e'd five chances, an' 'e 'ad;
'E's wounded, killed, and pris'ner, all the lot,
The bloody lot all rolled in one. Jim's mad.

Wilfred Owen

Casualty

They bring us crushed fingers,
mend it, doctor.
They bring burnt-out eyes,
hounded owls of hearts,
they bring a hundred white bodies,
a hundred red bodies,
a hundred black bodies,
mend it, doctor,
on the dishes of ambulances they bring
the madness of blood
the scream of flesh,
the silence of charring,
mend it, doctor.

And while we are suturing
inch after inch,
night after night,
nerve to nerve,
muscle to muscle,
eyes to sight,
they bring in
even longer daggers,
even more thunderous bombs,
even more glorious victories,

idiots.

Miroslav Holub

translated by Ewald Osers

Fifteen million plastic bags

I was walking in a government warehouse
Where the daylight never goes.
I saw fifteen million plastic bags
Hanging in a thousand rows.

Five million bags were six feet long
Five million bags were five foot five
Five million were stamped with Mickey Mouse
And they came in a smaller size.

Were they for guns or uniforms
Or a dirty kind of party game?
Then I saw each bag had a number
And every bag bore a name.

And five million bags were six feet long
Five million were five foot five
Five million were stamped with Mickey Mouse
And they came in a smaller size.

So I've taken my bag from the hanger
And I've pulled it over my head
And I'll wait for the priest to zip it
So the radiation won't spread.

Now five million bags are six feet long
Five million are five foot five
Five million are stamped with Mickey Mouse
And they come in a smaller size.

Adrian Mitchell

General, your tank is a powerful vehicle

General, your tank is a powerful vehicle.
It smashes down forests and crushes a hundred men.
But it has one defect:
It needs a driver.

General, your bomber is powerful.
It flies faster than a storm and carries more than an elephant.
But it has one defect:
It needs a mechanic.

General, man is very useful.
He can fly and he can kill.
But he has one defect:
He can think.

Bertolt Brecht

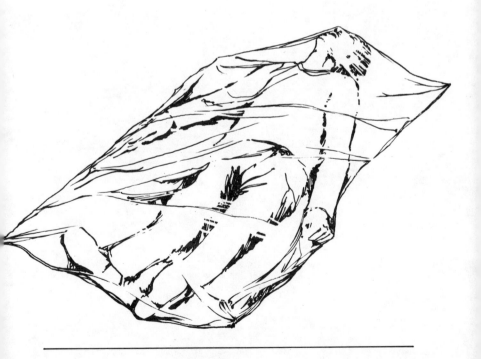

Atrocities

You told me, in your drunken-boasting mood,
How once you butchered prisoners. That was good!
I'm sure you felt no pity while they stood
Patient and cowed and scared, as prisoners should.

How did you do them in? Come, don't be shy:
You know I love to hear how Germans die,
Downstairs in dug-outs. 'Camerad!' they cry;
Then squeal like stoats when bombs begin to fly.

And you? I know your record. You went sick
When orders looked unwholesome: then, with trick
And lie, you wangled home. And here you are,
Still talking big and boozing in a bar.

Siegfried Sassoon

Life ending

The collier's wife

Somebody's knockin' at th' door
  Mother, come down an' see!
—I's think it's nobbut a beggar;
  Say I'm busy.

It's not a beggar, mother; hark
  How 'ard 'e knocks!
—Eh, tha'rt a mard-arsed kid,
  'E'll gie thee socks!

Shout an' ax what 'e wants,
  I canna come down.
—'E says, is it Arthur Holliday's?
  —Say Yes, tha clown.

'E says: Tell your mother as 'er mester's
  Got hurt i' th' pit—
What? Oh my Sirs, 'e never says that,
  That's not it!

Come out o' th' way an' let me see!
  Eh, there's no peace!
An' stop thy scraightin', childt,
  Do shut thy face!

'Your mester's 'ad a accident
  An' they ta'ein' 'im i' th' ambulance
Ter Nottingham.'—Eh dear o' me,
  If 'e's not a man for mischance!

Wheer's 'e hurt this time, lad?
  —I dunna know,
They on'y towd me it wor bad—
  It would be so!

Out o' my way, childt! dear o' me, wheer
  'Ave I put 'is clean stockin's an' shirt?
Goodness knows if they'll be able
  To take off 'is pit-dirt!

An' what a moan 'e'll make! there niver
  Was such a man for a fuss
If anything ailed 'im; at any rate
  I shan't 'ave 'im to nuss.

I do 'ope as it's not so very bad!
  Eh, what a shame it seems
As some should ha'e hardly a smite o' trouble
  An' others 'as reams!

It's a shame as 'e should be knocked about
  Like this, I'm sure it is!
'E's 'ad twenty accidents, if 'e's 'ad one;
  Owt bad, an' it's his!

There's one thing, we s'll 'ave a peaceful 'ouse
    f'r a bit,
Thank heaven for a peaceful house!
An' there's compensation, sin' it's accident.
  An' club-money—I won't growse.

An' a fork an' a spoon 'e'll want—an' what else?
I s'll never catch that train!
What a traipse it is, if a man gets hurt!
I sh'd think 'e'll get right again.

                    D. H. Lawrence

Death of a son

Yes, Joe died, my oldest son, he died.

. He got hurt one morning and he died
at eight o'clock that night same day.
He got hurt just over there where our fence
follows the old highway.

He was work for Hargreave's Ranch that time.
He tied his lunch on the saddle and got up on this horse
and went look for cattle down toward Deep Creek, yes.
Cattle used to roam all over the country, you know.

But he didn't make it, no, he didn't make it.

This horse he had it was still quite wild.
It didn't fully understand the bridle yet.
If you pull it too hard, it used to fall back.
It you spurred it, it would straighten out.

But he didn't have spurs on, no, he didn't have spurs.

I was packing water from the spring 'way down the hill.
I heard someone yell; I heard him calling me.
I dropped my buckets and I ran, my God!
I ran through high grass and bush; I fell, I ran and fell again.

I found him lying there in the grass, yes, I found him.

I don't know just what really happened.
I think this wild horse wanted to cross the fence
to our other horses and he bolted or bucked
or jumped and fell—but I don't know really what happened.

Except Joe lay there with a hole in his head, yes, in his head.

Is what killed him, I guess. His lunch was smashed.
George threw it away and we took him down to hospital
at the Lake, but they couldn't do nothing.
He died at eight o'clock that night same day.

When I carry water from the spring sometimes
I hear him calling from over there. But he's not there, no.

I buried him at the Mission. I buried my son at the Mission.

Mary Augusta Tappage

Mother to son

Well, son, I'll tell you:
Life for me ain't been no crystal stair.
It's had tacks in it,
And splinters,
And boards torn up,
And places with no carpet on the floor—
Bare.
But all the time
I'se been a-climbin' on,
And reachin' landin's,
And turnin' corners,
And sometimes goin' in the dark
Where there ain't been no light.
So boy, don't you turn back.
Don't you set down on the steps
'Cause you finds it's kinder hard.
Don't you fall now—
For I'se still goin', honey,
I'se still climbin',
And life for me ain't been no crystal stair.

Langston Hughes

Note for the future

When I get old
don't dress me in
frayed jackets
and too-short trousers,
and send me out
to sit around bowling-greens
in summer.
Don't give me just enough
to exist on, and expect me
to like passing
the winter days
in the reading-room
of the local library, waiting
my turn to read
last night's local paper.
Shoot me!
Find a reason, any reason,
say I'm a troublemaker,
or can't take care of myself
and live in a dirty room.
If you're afraid
of justifying my execution
on those terms,
tell everyone I leer
at little girls, and then
shoot me!
I don't care why you do it,
but do it,
and don't leave me
to walk to corner-shops
counting my coppers,
or give me a pass to travel cheap
at certain times, like a leper.
Don't send me to a home
to sit and talk
about the weather.

I don't want free tours,
half-price afternoon film-shows,
and friendly visitors.
If I can't live in independence
get me when I'm sixty-five, and
shoot me, you bastards, shoot me!

Jim Burns

Follow-up section

The poems in this book are drawn from many different sources and many different kinds of writer. Here are some notes to help you follow up where some of them come from.

*Children's voices can be as powerful as adults'. That's why we've put in a good number (see the stars against their names in the Acknowledgements list). You might like to have a look at other collections of children's writing like *Children as Writers* (published every year by W. H. Smith and Heinemann); *Stepney Words 1 and 2*, (Centerprise), *City Lines*, (ILEA English Centre), *As good as we make it* (writing by Centerprise young writers).

*If you still haven't heard of Michael Rosen's poems for children then have a go at *Mind your own business* (Fontana Lion); *Wouldn't you like to know* (Puffin); *You come too* (with Roger McGough, Puffin); and *The Bakerloo Flea* (Longman Knockout).

Rabbiting on (Fontana Lion) and *Hot Dog and other poems* (Puffin) show Kit Wright dealing with children coping with grown-ups and feature the adventures of daring Dave Dirt.

*Barry Heath comes from near Mansfield in Nottinghamshire and he writes his poems down as he says them. More of his stuff can be found in *M'Mam sez* (Your Own Stuff Press).

*Spike Milligan's poems are a bit erratic but sometimes he hits the jackpot. Other books of his are *A book of Milliganimals* (Puffin), *A Dustbin of Milligan*, (Tandem Books); *Unspun socks from a Chicken's Laundry* (Puffin).

*The best collection of Roger McGough is *In the Glassroom* (Jonathan Cape). But *Sporting Relations* (Eyre Methuen), *Gig* and *After the merrymaking* (both Jonathan Cape) are also well worth having a look at.

*'A Rock Concert in Belfast' by Patrick Gibson comes from a collection of poems by young people from Northern Ireland called *The Scrake of Dawn* (Blackstaff Press, 3 Galway Park, Dundonald, Belfast). Another collection from Northern Ireland is *Under the Moon Over the stars* (Arts Council of Northern Ireland, Bedford House, Bedford Street, Belfast).

*Black writers – we've aimed at a wide range of different voices speaking from the heart of their own communities in their own ways. If you want to follow up black community writers see *Talking Blues* (Centerprise); *Bluefoot Traveller* (Harrap); the publications of Black Ink, 1 Gresham Road, Brixton, London S.W.9; *Going where the work is* by Isaac Gordon (Centerprise) and the entry on James Berry below.

*Sam Greenlee writes, 'My chief literary influences are Charlie Parker, Lester Young, Miles Davis and Billie Holliday. As a writer, I consider myself a jazz musician whose instrument is an Olivetti typewriter.' More blues and poems can be found in his *Ammunition! Poetry and other Raps* (Bogle-L'Ouverture Publications).

*Poems by young black writers aren't easy to come across. But there are three very good collections by individual writers: *Tall Thoughts* by Deepak Kalha (Basement Writers); *Poems* by Vivian Usherwood (Centerprise); *Poems* by Marisa Horsford (Your Own Stuff Press).

*Other poems by Miroslav Holub are worth pursuing. Try 'A Boy's Head' in *Voices: the Third Book* (Penguin) and 'A History Lesson' included in *Openings* (ed. McLeod, *The English Project*, Ward Lock Educational).

*You might like to follow up Adrian Mitchell's poems in his collected edition, *For Beauty Douglas: Collected Poems 1953–1979* (Allison and Busby). Some lively ones to look out for are 'A Tourist Guide to England', 'Old Age Report', 'Ten ways to avoid lending your wheelbarrow to anybody', 'Leaflets' and 'Most people ignore poetry'.

*Robert Froman has brought out a book of poems, *Seeing things* (Abelard) where the words *do* what they *mean*. Try and get hold of a copy of *Eclipse* by Alan Riddell (Calder and Boyars), or catch a glimpse of the shape poem section in *Touchstones 2* by M. and P. Benton (The English Universities' Press) for other examples.

*Langston Hughes is an American writer, strong on people talking in his poems. If you can't get hold of his *Selected Poems* (Alfred Knopf Inc.) through the inter-library loan scheme then why not write to or visit the Arts Council Poetry Library (105 Piccadilly, London W1) where they've got a copy that you can borrow.

*If you like the look and general feel of poems on the page then you might get something out of Ian Hamilton Finlay's beautifully printed *Honey by the water* (Black Sparrow Press, Los Angeles, USA). It's available in the Arts Council Poetry Library. See above.

*If you're interested in young women's writings after reading Robin Morgan, Michelene Wandor or Liz Lochhead then it's worth having a look at *Up-Beat* by Michelene Wandor and others (Journeyman Press) *The Twelve-Spoked Wheel Flashing* by Marge Piercy (Alfred Knopf, New York) *Two-Headed Poems* by Margaret Atwood (Simon and Schuster, New York) and a collection of articles and stories edited by Susan Hemmings, *Girls are powerful* (Sheba Feminist Publishers). For more about Liz Lochhead see below.

Bricklight: Poems from the Labour Movement in East London edited by Chris Searle (Pluto Press) takes a view of the world from below like Sally Flood's poem, 'A working mum'. For more Sally Flood see *Paper Talk* (Basement Writers).

*Liz Lochhead is a Glasgow writer who's particularly sharp on exploring the fresh choices open to girls about who they are and who they might be. Her collections are *Memo for Spring* (Reprographia, 23 Livingstone Place, Edinburgh); *Islands* (Print Studio Press, Glasgow); *The Grimm Sisters* (Next Editions/Faber and Faber).

*You've got to hear John Cooper Clarke, the Manchester Punk poet, spit the words out in one of his whirlwind performances to really get the most out of what he's talking about. Try and listen to some of the tracks on 'Me and my big mouth', 'Snap, crackle and bop' and 'Walking back to happiness' (all Epic Records) before you read some more of his poems from *Directory 1979* (Omnibus Press) and *Ten years in an open-necked shirt* (Arena Arrow/Hutchinson 1983).

*If you rummage through Bertolt Brecht's *Poems 1913-1956* (Eyre Methuen) there are all kinds of worthwhile surprises. Find 'Burial of the trouble-maker in a zinc coffin', 'Questions from a worker who reads', 'Travelling in a comfortable car', 'Children's crusade', 'Six late Theatre poems'.

*'I've been more and more interested, since I started writing, in exploring the actual speech-sounds I hear and use myself . . .' So says Tom Leonard, another neglected Glasgow writer. His stuff is mostly in little magazines like *Bunnit Husslin* (Third Eye publication, Glasgow), *Ghostie Men* (Galloping Dog Press, 3 Otterburn Terrace, Newcastle upon Tyne), but the best of his speaking voice poems can be found in the 'Six Glasgow poems' included in *Poems* (E. and T. O'Brien Ltd, 11 Clare Street, Dublin 2), and *Three Glasgow writers* (Molendinar Press, 73 Robertson Street, Glasgow G2).

*Many people forget that D. H. Lawrence wrote a handful of poems that use the movement of common speech. They can be found in the *Complete Poems* (ed. Sola Pinto and Warren Roberts, Penguin). Try 'Violets', 'Whether or not' and some of the snappy 'Pansies'.

*The Caribbean voice is well caught by James Berry in his collections, *Fractured Circles* (New Beacon Books) and *Cut-Way Feelins Loving and Lucy's Letters* (Strange Lime Fruit Stone, Stafford-London). The gossipy exchange between women in the Caribbean and London, used in *Lucy's Letters*, is particularly worth discovering.

Poetry books for the classroom library

Strictly Private ed. Roger McGough, Puffin Plus
Many People, Many Voices ed. Norman Hidden, Hutchinson
Salford Road Gareth Owen, Kestrel
Swings and Roundabouts Mick Gowar, Collins
Bluefoot Traveller ed. James Berry, Harrap
Hot Dog and other poems Kit Wright, Puffin
Talking Blues, Centerprise, 136 Kingsland High Street, London E8
Where the sidewalk ends Shel Silverstein, Harper and Row
City Lines ILEA English Centre, Sutherland Street, London S.W.1
M'Mam sez Barry Heath, Your Own Stuff Press, 18 Waterloo Road, Beeston, Nottingham
Children as Writers (published each year) Heinemann/W. H. Smith
Mind your own business Michael Rosen, Fontana Lion
In the Glassroom Roger McGough, Jonathan Cape
Tall Thoughts Deepak Kalha, Basement Writers, Old Town Hall, Cable Street, London E1
The Penguin Book of Oral Poetry ed. Ruth Finnegan, Penguin
Englan is a bitch Linton Kwesi Johnson, Race Today Publications
Voices (the publication of the Worker Writers and Community Publishers), 61 Bloom Street, Manchester M1 3LY
The Grimm Sisters Liz Lochhead, Next Editions/Faber and Faber
Terry Street Douglas Dunn, Faber and Faber
Poems Vivian Usherwood, Centerprise
Poems 1913–1956 Bertolt Brecht, Eyre Methuen
Fractured Circles James Berry, New Beacon Books
Seeing things Robert Froman, Abelard Schuman
The Complete Poems D. H. Lawrence, Penguin
Poems Marisa Horsford, Your Own Stuff Press
The Penguin Book of Women poets ed. Cosman, Keefe and Weaver, Penguin
I see a voice ed. Michael Rosen, Hutchinson/Thames TV

Index of Authors

AGARD, Sandra 98
ANON 43, 58, 63

BALLENTINE, Keith 11
BARNES, William 33
BERRY, James 90
BLACKETT, Pamela 102
BOATSWAIN, Hugh 48
BRECHT, Bertolt 82, 111
BROWN, Pete 38
BURNS, Jim 115

CARNEGIE, Debbie 9
CARUANA, Sunny 17
CASEY, Mary 84
CHAPLIN, Alex 28
CLARK, John Cooper 74
COLLYMORE, Frank 94
CRANSWICK, Helen 15

ELLIS, Judith 40

FARQUARSON, Cassandra 106
FINLAY, Ian Hamilton 44
FLOOD, Sally 70
FROMAN, Robert 30, 72, 105

GIBSON, Patrick 46
GORDON, Isaac 20
GOWAR, Mick 60
GREENLEE, Sam 49, 52
GUARD, Philip 100

HARBOTTLE, Anita 97
HEATH, Barry 14, 41, 92
HOLUB, Miroslav 26, 109
HUGHES, Langston 31, 54, 80, 104, 114

JACKSON, Alan 95

KALHA, Deepak 22

LAING, R.D. 62
LAWRENCE, D.H. 101, 116
LEONARD, Tom 39, 85
LIPSITZ, Lou 79
LOCHHEAD, Liz 32, 64, 68
LOCKWOOD, Dai 73
LOWELL, Amy 96

MARKMAN, Stephanie 67
MARTIN, Carol 93
MCGOUGH, Roger 18, 37
MILLIGAN, Spike 16
MITCHELL, Adrian 28, 75, 78, 86, 110
MORGAN, Robin 66

OWEN, Wilfred 108

PAYNE, Michael 47
PEARCE, Bobby 99
PORTER, Rose 36
POSTGATE, Margaret 106
PRITCHARD, Adam 59

ROSEN, Michael 10, 24, 34, 61

SANDBURG, Carl 103
SASSOON, Siegfried 112
SCANNELL, Vernon 77
SERRAILLIER, Ian 42
SLAVIN, Helen 76
STIVEN, Tessa 51

TAKUBOKU, Ishikawa 40
TAPPAGE, Mary Augusta 81, 118

WANDOR, Michelene 65
WILLIAMS, Frederick 56
WRIGHT, Kit 12

Acknowledgements

Photographs by courtesy of Sally and Richard Greenhill, except for page 78 which is from Keystone Press Agency.

The editors and publishers wish to thank the following who have kindly given permission for the use of copyright material:

Allison & Busby Ltd for 'Wages' by Alan Jackson; Andium Press for 'A Note for the Future' from *A Single Flower* by Jim Burns; Associated Book Publishers Ltd for two extracts from *Poems 1913-1956* by Bertolt Brecht, 'General, Your Tank' translated by Lee Baxendall, and 'A Worker's Speech to a Doctor' translated by Frank Jellinek; Blackstaff Press Ltd for 'A Rock Concert in Belfast' by Patrick Gibson from *The Scrake of Dawn;* Bogle-L'Ouverture Publications Ltd for 'Blues for Stevie Wonder' and 'Immigrants' by Sam Greenlee from *Ammunition*; CBS Songs Ltd for 'majorca' by John Cooper Clarke; Jonathan Cape Ltd for 'Dumb Insolence' and 'Saw it in the Papers' by Adrian Mitchell from *The Apeman Cometh,* 'Early Shift on the Evening Standard News Desk' and 'Under Photographs of Two Party Leaders Smiling' by Adrian Mitchell from *Ride the Nightmare* and 'Fifteen Million Plastic Bags' by Adrian Mitchell from *Poems*; 'A Letter of Application' by Anita Harbottle from *Firewords* by Chris Searle; 'Napoleon' by Miroslav Holub, translated by Ian and Jarmila Milner, from *Although*; and 'First Day at School' and 'Nooligan' from *In the Classroom* by Roger McGough; Laura Casey for 'The Class Game' by the late Mrs Mary Casey; Wm Collins Sons & Co. Ltd for 'Would You Believe It' from *Swings and Roundabouts.* Copyright © 1981 by Mick Gower; Helen Cranswick* for 'Mum, can I go out?'; Douglas & McIntyre Ltd for 'The One They Took' and 'Death of a Son' by Mary Augusta Tappage from *The Days of Augusta,* edited by Jean E. Speare; The English Centre for the poem 'The Production Line' by Bobby Pearce* from *City Lines*; Philip Guard* for 'My Dad These Days'; Hackney Reading Centre on behalf of the authors for 'School' by Isaac Gordon* from *Going Where the Work Is* and 'Dub Rock' by Hugh Boatswain* and 'The Careers Interview' by Sandra Agard* from *Talking Blues*; Harcourt Brace Jovanovich Inc. for 'The Hangman at Home' from *Smoke and Steel* by Carl Sandburg; Barry Heath for 'bacon rind', 'ee shynta ducked' and 'Guy Fawkes' from *M'Mam Sez*; Heinemann Educational Books for 'More Haste – Less Speed' by Pamela Blackett from *Young Writers: 23rd Year*; Kodansha International/USA for 'Accidentally' by Ishikawa Takuboku from *Poems to Eat*; Stephanie Markman for 'The Male Tradition'; Carol Martin* for 'Removal from Glengall Grove'; Hughes Massie Ltd on behalf of the estate of Langston Hughes for 'Delinquent', 'Ballad of the Landlord' and 'Green Memory' from *Selected Poems of Langston Hughes*; Spike Milligan Productions Ltd for 'The Dog Lovers' by Spike Milligan; New Beacon Books Ltd for 'From Lucy: Carnival' from *Fractured Circles* by James Berry;

Ewald Osers for his translation of 'Casualty' by Miroslav Holub; Penguin Books Ltd for extracts from *Do You Love Me?* by R. D. Laing (Penguin Books, 1977), copyright © 1976 by R.D. Laing, and 'Hugger mugger' from *Hot Dog and Other Poems* by Kit Wright (Kestrel Books 1981), text copyright © 1981 by Kit Wright; Random House Inc. for 'Madam and the Census Man' and 'Mother to Son' from *Selected Poems of Langston Hughes*; George Sassoon for 'Atrocities' from *The War Poems* by Siegfried Sassoon; Vernon Scannell for 'Dusk Jockey'; Ian Serraillier for 'No Swimming in the Town' from *I'll Tell You a Tale* published by Puffin and Kestrel Books. Copyright © 1973 by Ian Serraillier; Michelene Wandor for 'Let us Now Praise Fearful Men'; A. P. Watt Ltd on behalf of Robert Froman for 'Wall Walk', 'Development' and 'Madness' from *Seeing Things* by Robert Froman; Wesleyan University Press for 'Skinny Poem' by Lou Lipsitz from *Cold Water*. Copyright © 1966 by Lou Lipsitz.

Every effort has been made to trace all the copyright holders but if any have been inadvertently overlooked the publishers will be pleased to make the necessary arrangement at the first opportunity.

* Child writer